Personal statement

Always believe in yourself and never give up on your dreams.
Hard work pays off for those who do not tire out.

 www.trafford.com

North America & international
toll-free: 844-688-6899 (USA & Canada)
fax: 812 355 4082

Dedication

I would like to dedicate this book of poems to God for giving me
The talent to write poetry, and also my mom for raising me .

Introduction

The poetry of today has hardly received its due need of appreciation,
As time goes by hopefully people will start to appreciate this beautiful
Language and embraced it for it contains the power to change lives and
Offers hope. A revelation to all those seeking .

TABLE OF CONTENTS

Destiny

From out of the shadows and into the light ,
I have come to take my position so I do stand upright.
I must admit it has been long over due,
But ,now I am here right among all of you.
So witness my come back with motion and stride,
It is my time now to blossom and shine.
Like a prince my reign will be in royalty,
It is the season for me to rise at full peak.
In splendor and glory so everyone can see,
That indeed that this really is my true destiny.
So now I shall arise with the power of the sun,
On the world with my poetry with a message for everyone.
No matter what the nationality hair of skin color,
I have come with a message to share with all others

The end.

Lady

If I had one more chance I would do things right,
Maybe then lady you would be by my side.
Deep down in my heart I know I did you wrong,
I'm sorry ,but its too late and now you are gone.
At night I cry with the thoughts of losing you,
Now I am alone in this big old empty room.
I look out my window hoping to see your face,
Standing by the door and calling my name.
Come back home cause I miss you so much,
The way we used to kiss and the way we touched.
I can't imagine living my life without you,
All my days now are so cold and so blue.
Now all I have are my deepest memories,
Of how it use to be between you and me.
I had hoped one day that to me you would return,
And set my spirit free like one does a bird.
You have moved on now and let me be,
I always will remember you my dear lady.

The end.

Real love

Love can neither be bought nor sold,
It has to come from your heart within your soul.
Worth more than gold a true commodity,
That will last a lifetime throughout all eternity.
Whether good or bad times real love still exists,
It has a purpose and that is to stay in your midst.
To comfort you and to give you hope,
A strong reassurance to never let go.
Hold on to love cause it is a special thing,
A gift from God who knows what we need.
If you have found it then you are truly blessed,
I can't think of anything else that equals to it.
A real treasure love is with its own rewards,
Something each person individual longs for.
To find somebody that makes them feel this way,
Now and forever together for always.

The end.

My prayer

Dear God please hear my prayer,
Thank you for this day of life for it I treasure.
You know me better than anyone else,
Even better than I know my own self.
You have been with me through my ups and downs,
Gave me strength when no one was around.
You cared for me when no one else did,
And gave me a reason to hope and live.
Thank you God for being my friend,
You stayed by my side and never gave in.
You taught me how to love all over again,
Your word is salvation to every woman and man.
My faith in you will never dry out,
Your word refreshes me like water for the mouth.
Teach me your laws so others I may tell,
About your greatness and power to this I swear.
You're loving and kind with faithfulness,
The beauty of your strength brings awe in mightiness.
Dear God my savior yes you are,
Because of you I can see wide and far.
Thank you God for watching over me ,
A better man you have made me to be.
Through the mercy and sacrifice of Jesus I pray,
To remember all that you have done for me amen.

The end.

A gentleman's cue

My dear lady so sweet and so fine,
How I long to make you all mine.
I think of you every day and each night,
There is no place I'd rather be than by your side.
To comfort you and to be your true love,
I'll hold you in my arms now and forever more.
Your pain I will heal and those tears I will catch,
Please give me a chance that is all I ask.
To be with you would be a dream come true,
I must admit I do love you.
So don't be shy for I mean you no harm,
There is no need for fear nor cause for alarm.
A gentleman's cue is what I have written today,
For someone special that makes me feel this way.
Oh you beautiful woman your eyes are like the stars,
Your face shines like the moon I always know where you are.
A precious gift you are that money can't buy,
You're worth more than pearls a real treasure for all time.
I hope and pray that you may truly understand,
As you read these words I wrote with my own two hands.
Oh dear woman you bring out the best in me,
I just had to let you know so why can't you see.

The end.

Emotions

I cannot hide sometimes the way that I feel,
My body itself knows my despair and on my face it is revealed.
My mind is the trigger and the heart is the receiver,
Together they bring pain making my whole frame weaker,
Deep inside my soul I feel so much emptiness,
It is hard to adjust sometimes surrounded by loneliness.
Inside I am crying and nobody can hear,
The weight of the whole world on my shoulders I do feel.
I am alone with no one to confide in,
That will truly understand all of these things.
Like a man on a raft lost way out at sea,
So am I although my physical you see.
Trapped from within with no apparent escape,
Haunted by mixed feelings I stomach each day.

The end.

Man

Created in the image of God I am,
Although flesh and blood on earth I do stand.
Given the breath of life by him I came to be,
A living soul a truly precious being.
Two eyes, two ears, a nose and a mouth,
Two hands, two feet that is something to think about.
Designed perfectly in every aspect and detail,
From the smallest to the greatest he made me well.
A brain he gave to support our functions,
I have to admit that God is really something.
Every ligament and bone is in its rightful space,
Along with each organ and vessel assigned to there place.
We breathe and skip about without worry or fear,
For God is our designer and great engineer.
As a confession to you I have to make this day,
Yes indeed I am wonderfully made.

The end.

Untitled

Roses are red and violets are blue,
How colorful you are so blossom in bloom.
Like a lamp you shine so that everyone can see,
How beautiful you are from your head down to your feet.
Your eyes are like diamonds bright and crystal clear,
That sparkle throughout the land whenever you are near.
The hair on your head is like that of gold straw,
So precious and valuable to preserve forever more.
Your lips are like plums so round and so sweet,
Like a magnet you attract giving sparks to everything.
Like and angel you are flowing in the wind,
No one can compare to the elegance you send.
Your style and rhythm are truly unique,
Unlike anything at all that I have ever seen.
The talk of the town and everybody knows your name,
With dignity and splendor every man you have tamed.
All hats are off to you because respect is your middle name,
A super woman you are deserving of all the fame.
It is a privilege for me to be graced with your presence,
And witness the marvelous display of your essence.
Oh woman with you is the key to happiness,
The power you have to unlock any door that you wish.
Any man would be proud to have you as his wife,
To love and to cherish and hold each night.

The end.

Homeless

Can anyone spare a quarter or a dime,
I haven't ate all day full of hunger am I.
Alone I sit in a corner by a wall,
People stop and look ,but give nothing at all.
My head I lay low in agony and shame,
Deep inside my heart it is to God I pray.
To watch over me for all my friends ran away,
When I really needed help by my side no one stayed.
A pair of pants and a shirt is all that I have,
A single pair of shoes and one small bag.
It is cold on the outside trying to look in,
At a time like this I wish I had one good friend.
To take me in for a home cook meal,
A shower would be nice I miss how that feels.
Life is hard for me now I suffer each day,
I'm on bending knees from the pain I do face.
Searching as I do for a place to lay down,
To rest my head and hope to be found.
At night I look up into the sky above,
I ask God is it me that he is thinking of.
I know that he will not forsake me,
It just seems like forever out here in these streets.

The end.

Forgiveness

If someone sins against us are we willing to forgive,
Or do we lash back in anger or in a fit.
It isn't easy at all to turn the other cheek,
We have to pray for others who still may be weak.
Christ Jesus paved the way when he came down to earth,
So follow his example yes even for all sinners.
Our reward will be in heaven for God knows very well,
Good job faithful slave out to you he will yell.
So open up your heart and learn to forgive,
Hold no grudges show mercy and continue innocent.

The end.

Dedication

Dear mom,

I can remember my child hood like it was just yesterday,
I can still hear my mom's voice echo my name.
To wash my face and get ready for dinner,
To say my prayer and be thankful for what I was eating.
You raised me from a boy to a man,
Gave me guidance when I needed a hand.
Through my ups and downs you comforted me,
An ankle of support to hold securely.
A role model you are with footsteps to follow,
I want to be just like you someday when I am a father.
Thanks Mom for being there for me,
Without you by my side just where would I be.
My best friend in the world you certainly are,
Cause of you love I now can see far.

The end..

Mountains

So huge and very tall,
They stand erect and yet do not fall.
A marvel to gaze upon a sight for all eyes,
A public declaration to the world they cry.
Perfectly designed in every detail,
From height to depth they were made really well.
Created for our pleasure with the purpose to enjoy,
All of their Splendor we just simply adore.
A language they speak in there own special way,
We can only imagine what it is they would say.
Mountains picture more than just a thousand words,
They capture our imagination so high up above.

The end.

One in a million

You are the key in my life that unlocks the door for me,
My inspiration to achieve my hopes and my dreams.
More valuable than gold and precious than silver,
My soul and heart you have captured and clinch
A comfort zone that guides my every step,
To break my fall whether right or left.
A place to hide when it rains or storms,
A blanket of love that keeps me warm.
A shadow that walks right next to me,
A friend to me in times of need.
You are my everything and so much more,
Because of you in my life I now have joy.
You have filled my world with so much happiness,
I must admit that you are heaven-sent.

The end.

Night watch

Most likely on any given night,
One can look up and catch a beautiful sight.
A baby blue sky with moon and stars,
Lighting up the night no matter where you are.
Like a picture painted perfect they seem to excel,
There is a sense of peace and calm everywhere.
Our moods they enhance like music to the soul,
Stimulating our minds they seize and unfold.
A melody they play as each one performs each night,
Demonstrating to the world they also have life.
Without question or doubt they stand to be recognized,
By each individual who looks up into the sky.

The end.

CROSS ROADS

Today in our life we face many challenges,
Sometimes the road gets rough even hard to handle them.
No matter what it may be our goal is to never give up,
Even if you fall down you must get back up.
A person is only strong as he allows himself to be,
 If you have faith then you truly will succeed.
To go out and conquer whatever it is,
To take control over your whole life once again.
Confidence is something that you will surley have,
Now that you are focus and headed down the right path.
The road ahead will be much more clearer,
Since you have faced your obstacles and changed the conditions.

The end.

Paradise soon

Last night I fell asleep and had the most unusual dream,
I was dressed in fine linen white and very clean.
As I looked around I saw people everywhere,
From all nations and tongues singing without despair.
So I ask the man who sat across from me,
Exactly where was I he said the Garden of Eve.
At that I stood up and what did I see,
A crystal blue sea that was clear as could be.
A rainbow that covered the whole entire earth,
Lighting up the sky with beautiful colors.
The land was good just like milk and honey,
There was plenty of food and no one was hungry.
The animals themselves seemed to be at peace with man,
Not a violent thing occurred or happened in that land.
War was gone for hate had vanished,
Replaced with love which sprinkled the whole planet.
So I ask the man when would these things really be,
Cause the world I live in we're still suffering.
He said to me that soon God would come,
To rescue man from all the damage being done.
To give hope to man cause he needs a savior,
And stop the pain and make things stable.
At that I woke up with a smile on my face,
Knowing soon the future for mankind would be safe.

The end.

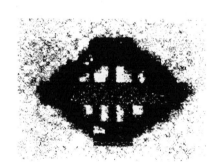

The almighty tongue

It has the power to build up or even put down,
Depending on the words we choose which come out our mouth.
Although a small member it can sting like a belt,
Causing a heart and spirit to wither or melt.
It can leave a person empty in silence to moan,
Our words carry weight like large stones.
Our speech can leave a mark for a very long time,
Leaving a scar or a smile into that other person's eye.
Everybody has feelings and they want to be treated the same,
It is not a lot to ask for on any giving day.
Be wise in your actions as to what you might say,
It can have a great impact on a person's physical state.

The end.

(song)   looking for love

(verse 1)   Girl look at the way how he disrespects you he don't deserve you
                I'm the type of guy that will be all faithful.

(pre-chorus) I can see it in your eyes he makes you sad and blue
              just give me a chance oh girl to satisfy you.

(chorus 1)   cause your looking for love so will you holla at me,
              your looking for love so will you holla at me,
               your looking for love so will you holla at me lady ah yeah.

(verse 2)   I know how you feel inside and what you are going through
              you gave him your heart and he turned his back on you
               he made you cry all night feeling like a fool
              I'll never do you wrong girl I will be there for you.

(chorus 2)   cause your looking for love so will you holla at me
               your looking for love so will you holla at me
              your looking for love so will you holla at me lady ah yeah

(bridge 1   Girl I will do anything to make you feel so special
               with you is where I wanna be for now and ever
               so tell me girl can we really work it out
              you know how I feel about you there is no doubt

(chorus 3)   cause your looking for love so will you holla at me
               your looking for love so will you holla at me
               your looking for love so will you holla at me lady ah yeah

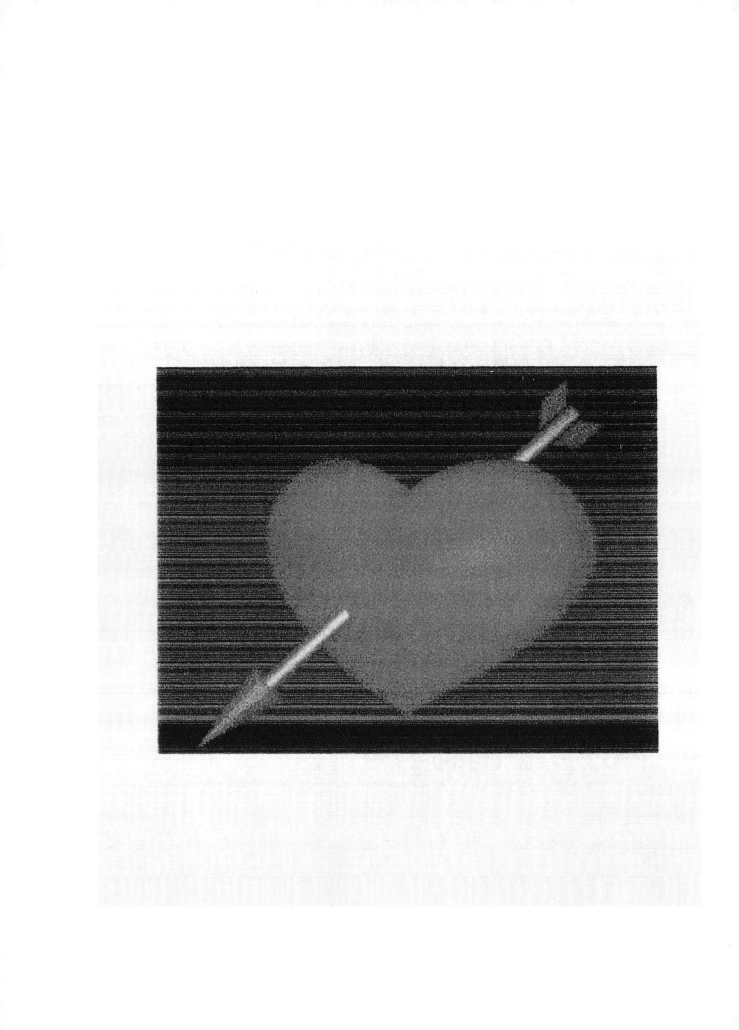

(song) remember

Baby you know what you did to me was wrong
You turned your back on me and our little home
You made your choice when you walk out the door
To pursue a life with out me in it no more

I feel so bad deep down inside my heart
You left with him and forgot your vows
I can't believe that you would do me wrong
After all I've done for you and now your gone
What about our life and all the things we shared
Did you think about it when you packed your bags

Just remember that I loved you girl
Please remember that I loved you girl

Was it really worth losing me
I guess our love didn't mean a thing
Are you sure he will be there for you
Or leave your heart sad and blue
Will he do you like the way you did me
I quess in time girl we will see
I'm long gone now so forget about me
That is just the way I feel it has to be

Just remember that I loved you girl
Please remember that I loved you girl

Baby you know what you did to me was wrong
You turned your back on me and our little home
You made your choice when you walked out the door
To pursue a life with out me in it no more

Survivor

I have the ambition so I will not tire out,
My mind I have focus to endure any storm or drought.
I channel all my energy and summoned up my strength,
To balance out my thoughts to continue each length.
Every move I have calculated and the distance I know,
I have prepared my body mentally for my journey ahead to go.
In harmony with my spirit my physical does flow,
Allowing me to operate and endure on my own.
The light within me can see so the darkness I avoid,
Enabling me to travel without resistance to my soul.
My path for me is set with no errors at all,
My direction is confirmed by my persistents not to fall.
A strong will plus faith keeps all my hope alive,
Giving me the edge in order for me to survive.

The end.

Church

Friend

A true friend is someone you can always count on,
Who will stand by your side and never do you wrong.
A companion to you in times of need,
A shoulder to hold on and cry in sincerity and freely.
A refuge of comfort showing you love with honesty,
Truly understanding your feelings and emotions totally.
Always patient listening to what you have to say,
Never harsh or abusive showing love to you in every way.
They always know the right words to you to convey,
To lift up your spirits and to make your day.
Through the ups and downs they are by your side always,
A real true friend whether night or day.

The end.

War

No matter who wins the war both sides still suffer,
The lost of human life has to make everyone wonder.
Is there another way we can work our differences out,
Instead of bloodshed and destruction rampaging about.
Costing millions in repairs with money we don't have,
We could be feeding the poor people hungry in the land.
If we could just sit down for once and figure out a solution,
I guarantee there would be peace with harmony and union.
All nations working together for the sake of all man,
Not isolated in their ideas giving out a helping hand.
A lot can be accomplished if we all worked together,
War interrupts that effort and our plans to endeavor.

The end.

Hands of time

Sometimes I wish I could go back into the past,
To enjoy once again all the fond memories that I had.
In those days people really knew how to have a good time,
We made out with what we had and learned to be satisfied.
It was not about the money or being first in line,
It was about honor and trust on which people relied.
There was unity and strength and the people looked out for each other,
Your neighbor was a sister or even a brother.
If you needed a hand someone would help you out,
Without expecting anything in return setting no price amount.
Our house was not a prison that we felt trapped in,
The thought of being assaulted we never imagine.
There was work for all and no one was laid off,
We had a sense of security that nothing would fall.
Our attitude was broad and life was clear,
Not blurred like today with so much fear.
Our era was special people really lived back then,
There was hope in our future without darkness or mist.

The end.

Lonely

Oh loneliness please don't get the best of me,
My days are long slow and excruciating
Every breath that I take seems to wear me right down,
Because of the sadness in my heart of being push to the ground.
I feel so empty with no life at all,
Cornered by silence and only four walls.
I have no one at all that really cares about me,
I am constantly followed by grief and misery.
Which drain me of my power and all my energy ,
I feel so neglected and I cry in my sleep.
I need someone by my side to hold and comfort me,
To erase all this pain of which I speak.
Who can help me reverse this lonely dry spell,
And give me joy so the world I can tell.

The end

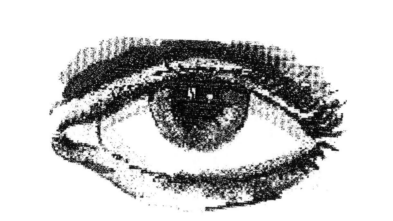

Eyes

If you looked into my eyes then my pain you would see,
It is not a secret at that I cry so profusely.
My eyes tell a story of heartbreak and sadness,
About a life of no justice neglect and abandonment.
The luster in my eyes have lost there light,
Due to the overwhelming conditions that I cannot hide.
They have become so heavy because of all my sighing,
Irritated and red from sleepless nights.
Watery and puffy and so very tense,
On account of the pain inflicted on them.
Leaving me uncomfortable and weary and so very weak,
Unable to stay focus and see clearly.
Causing me agony which makes me strain,
To open my eyes and see the light of the day.
The eyes indeed are the windows of the soul,
Like a mirror they reflect all our facial tones.

The end.

Sailing

On the ocean I am free like a bird who soars,
I am able to appreciate my surroundings even more.
It is calm out here so peaceful and quiet,
One can rest assured he can meditate in silence.
The wind blows occasionally a nice cool breeze,
And the sun does its job of energizing every living thing.
It is a feeling like no other something you have to try,
Out here one can feel free to relax his mind.
A chance to escape from the noise in the city,
A feeling of relief something we all have been missing.
To enjoy with our love ones or that special person in our lives,
A moment with nature to share and enjoy some quality time.
Surely something money simply cannot buy,
Serenity and harmony on the ocean that is alive.
The waves greet you and they sing their own song,
Welcoming you to participate and hum right along.
The setting is like a scene from a movie,
Only the special effects are real and they are so soothing.
So if you ever feel tired sad or even blue,
Set sail on the ocean it will refresh you.

The end.

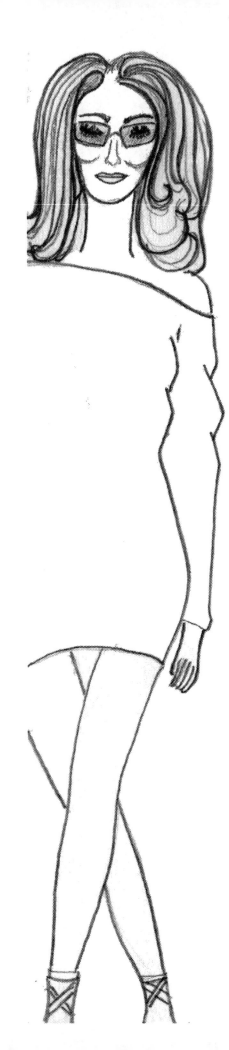

A woman's touch

A woman can ease a man's pain and calm his spirit,
She can even restrain a savage beast.
A woman has the power and strength of a nation,
And in her grasp is the key to life and salvation.
Although not a warrior she holds the symbol of justice,
And her love is the blanket that keeps out the cold.
Her passion is scented with incense and oils,
A healing to the body and even to the soul.
In wisdom she speaks her words could heal a bone,
Her touch restores the confidence for a man to believe totally.
A woman is the foundation and strength of every man,
Without her light it would be impossible for us to stand.
A woman is a precious gift given to a man,
To honor and respect and always cherish.
A woman's touch we do need here on this earth,
Her energy brings everything to life and it is beautiful.
Her zest for life can be seen in her eyes,
Without a doubt she is prepared to take care and provide.
Her foundation is solid and hard as concrete,
From her knowledge she builds on tranquility and peace.
A woman's touch we should never neglect,
Her power of reach exceeds far beyond our planet.

The end.

Guiding light

I am never lost at all in your presence,
My directions are accurate and are fully measured.
My path is laid out just like a map,
A blue print for success so there is no lapse.
With confidence I stand and I am able to succeed,
Because of my good navigator who taught me everything.
My anchor and protector who shields me from the dark,
And radiates my eyes so I will not get lost.
My guiding light who stands right next to me,
To make sure I am safe and in good health indeed.
So there is no need for me to worry or to fear,
Or be alarmed for my savior is near.
To help me at all times no matter where I may be,
My light of the world who shines down upon me.

The end.

True beauty

I see all the beauty of your heart when I look into your eyes,
Like a mirror they reflect all the love you have deep inside.
You are passionate and warm and so very sweet,
Your smile brightens up the room for all on lookers to see.
In a league of your own you stand and people recognize,
That you are something special which no man can deny.
When you talk people listen because they know you are sincere,
You care about other humans and that is what makes you so dear.
You lift the spirits of the weak and heal their pain,
By being a true friend through the thick and the thin.
On any giving day you are willing to lend a helping hand,
If someone needs assistance or is stuck in a jam.
You always say the right words that someone needs to hear,
When presented with difficulty or a problem real severe.
A shoulder to cry on whether day or night,
A tower of support that is secure and real tight.
An angel of God's from heaven you are,
That watches over his flock no matter near or far.
A role model you set for others to copy and follow,
By being and example and not being hollow,
 Clearing the fog and mist with hope for a better tomorrow.

The end.

Spiritual love

Deep inside my soul I feel you calling me,
I sense you are sincere and need me desperately.
You are my future love and my soul mate to be,
Our connection is equivalent to a burst of electricity.
And image of you I hold in my thoughts,
It is hard to explain so I listen to my heart.
Although far away where ever you may be,
I will hold you in my prayers to the day that we meet.
A love like this will never die out,
Because faith keeps us close to endure by the hour.
I know that you must feel the same way too,
Until we meet some days maybe cold or even blue.
Our paths will meet for it is our destiny to unite,
To come together as one to share a beautiful life.
As sure as the sun sets over the earth,
Our burning love will one day emerge.
So rest assured before it is said and done,
We will be together the two of us to form one.

The end.

Ebony queen

You are so beautiful and I am please to have you,
I like you the way you are so incredible and intellectual.
Your beauty still shines just like in the beginning of time,
Throughout the whole world your still recognize as truly divine.
Shower me with your love and hold me close,
Like the ancients did many years ago.
You are my queen and you make me feel so good,
I am your king and very please at what you do.
Hold over me the staff of your beaming light,
Like our ancestors once did in the thick of the night.
Comfort me with your strength and bless my seeds,
Teach them the law of God's promise to be.
Oh ebony queen answer my thirst for knowledge,
By reminding me of my duties and my alliance to God.
Stay by my side each and every single day,
Travel with me near or very far away.
I need you in my life like the earth needs water,
To live and breathe and continue to grow.
You are my source of strength and the reason why I conquer,
My key to victory amazing like no other.
Oh ebony queen you are my best friend,
Remain by my side so I can be blessed again and again.
In the ancient law it is written about you,
Your hair and your style and the wisdom you use.
Respect and honor is a must for you,
You deserve to be recognized for all the work you do.
The love of my heart the one that I have chosen,
To be apart of my life precious just like roses.
You are so beautiful am I am please to have you,
I have always admired everything you do.
I like the way that you are so incredible and intellectual,
Your words of thought heal me.
A natural you are and together we are complete,
You are the answer to my prayers.
The voice I listen to which makes me float,
You are my hero and so much more.
A special kind of woman who I truly adore,
God blessed me when he placed you in my life.

The end.

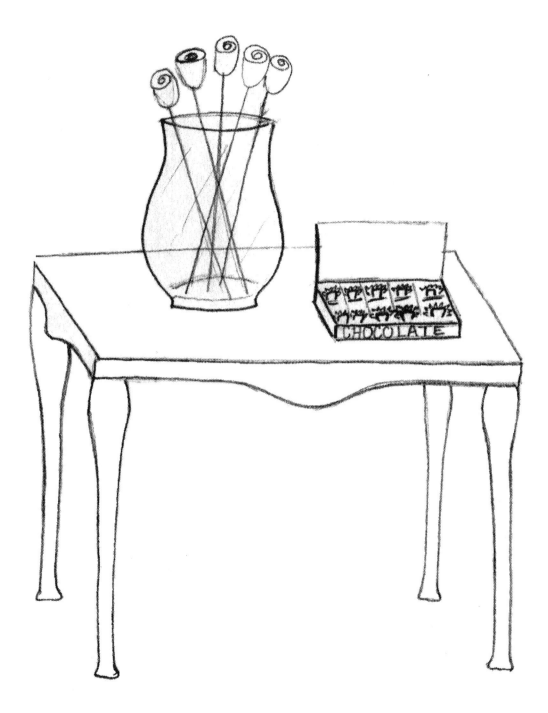

Serenade

Can I buy you flowers and chocolate my love and hold your hand,
Call you a queen like the royals in a distant land.
My dear I want to make you feel so special,
I will leave no doubt in your mind that I am interested.
My objectivity is your desire to awaken the flame and bring back the fire,
Of passion excitement and ecstasy to last your lifetime all eternity.
I want to take you on a journey to lovers land explore the world you might have taken for
granted, you have been looking for love in all the wrong places with to many heartbreaks
What a sad situation. Can I walk with you and talk to you, and speak from my heart
Because it is the truth. I am head over heals lady for your love ,my dear you are the moon
and I am the sun. I will sing a song full of psalms for your ears only, and testify my
whole soul devotion. I promise to always be by your side, together we can
Stand divine. I need a woman like you and you need me , so let us share our world and
Make our life complete. I want to hold you in my arms and stare in your eyes, and tell
You honey there is no need to cry. Have faith dear lady and believe in me ,together
We can make this all a reality. I will be your prince in shinning armor ,the one to rescue
You right now. The joy of your life you finally found at last, no more sad times
Now it is time to laugh. The equation for you and I is truly mathematical , 360 degrees is
our line of channel. Pure and organic and genuine, a love like ours will stand the test
Of time. more deeper than the ocean and wider than the sea, so lets constitute this here
Love decree . between me and you and God above, and say our vows in the name of love.

The end.

ABOUT THE AUTHOR

Michael Lamont Johnson has been writing poetry since the age of seventeen.
He graduated from Dover Jr, Sr, high school in upstate New York where he
still resides. After several years of compiling his work he has now decided
to publish a book of poems which he feels will touch the lives of many
readers
Who appreciate this form of expression.

Printed in the United States
by Baker & Taylor Publisher Services